DESCRIBING SKILLS FOR KIDS WITH AUTISM & ASPERGER'S

SIX-MINUTE THINKING SKILLS

WORKBOOK

HAPPY FROG PRESS

Print ISBN 978-1-7752852-6-7

Happy Frog Press

www.HappyFrogPress.com

INTRODUCTION

Welcome to the **Six-Minute Thinking Skills** series. These workbooks are designed for busy parents and professionals who need easy-to-use and effective materials for working with learners who struggle with the language and thinking skills required for school success.

This workbook, **Describing Skills,** provides step-by-step activities to quickly build the ability to describe objects, people and events.

These expressive language skills can be challenging for children with Autism/Aspergers and for adults with aphasia or other cognitive issues.

Use this workbook to build or rebuild your learner's ability to quickly and precisely describe an object, a person or an event.

ABOUT THIS WORKBOOK

Key details of this workbook are:

- Suitable for 1-1 or classroom use

  This book can be used in a classroom or with a single learner.

- Gradually increments difficulty

  Learners begin with simple description tasks, which gradually increment as the book progresses. By the end, learners will use 5-10 sentences to provide detailed descriptions.

- No-prep. No extra materials required

  Everything needed is included in the book. You can get started right now

- Small chunks. Use any time

  Our worksheets are designed for 'six-minute sessions.' Anytime you have a spare moment, your learner can accomplish the next incremental step in their learning journey.

The ability to verbalize and describe their world is key for all learners. Whether it is describing an item they are looking for, recounting an incident that occurred to them, this workbook will ensure your learner has the ability to express their needs, concerns and interests.

Support your struggling speakers with this fun, engaging workbook that will build your learner's ability and confidence in this important skill.

HOW TO COACH A SIX-MINUTE SESSION

No student wants to spend extra time learning. Follow the guidelines in this section to promote efficient and motivating progress for your student.

1. Have a consistent and regular schedule

Consistency and regularity are vital if you want to reach a goal. So, choose a regular schedule for your six-minute sessions, get your learner's agreement and stick to it!

In a school setting, make this task a regular part of your students' day. In a home setting, aim for 3-4 times per week.

2. Devise a reward system

Working on skill deficits is hard work for any learner. Appreciate your student's effort by building in a reward system.

This may include a reward when a specific number of exercises are finished, when tasks are completed correctly on the first try, or whatever specific goal will encourage your learner at this point in their journey.

Remember to reward based on effort as well as correctness.

3. Scaffold then fade for success

As your learner encounters a new challenge, scaffold the task so your learner can be successful.

For example, if your student can't think of the category an ambulance belongs to, try giving alternatives, "Is it a vehicle or a fruit?"

Later in the same session, try the same example and/or a similar example without scaffolding. For example, add 'fire truck' to the list of tasks.

Your learner is ready to move on to the next page when they can achieve 80% success without scaffolding.

Keep in mind, the task words you present to your learner should be known to them. Your student may learn new words to describe the item/person/event, but the basic object should be known to them.

If there is an unknown word in the list, replace it with something your learner knows.

4. Don't write in the book

What? It's a workbook, isn't it?

Well, yes. But your student will learn more if you complete this workbook orally. Instead of writing the answer, require your learner to answer orally in complete sentences.

Your learner's brain will work hard, but he or she will develop skills that are immediately generalizable.

In fact, the best use of the workbook is for you to use it for notes.

- Identify any words done incorrectly and make sure to add a few similar words to try later.
- Cross out and replace words your learner does not know.
- For middle-school learners, add in a few words from their current science, socials or English lessons.

5. Require complete sentences & model alternatives

Make sure your learners provide complete sentences when answering the prompt.

For example, when giving the category for an item, your learner should answer: *An apple is a fruit*, rather than just saying *fruit*.

As the tasks become more challenging, feel free to model more natural constructions after your learner has given a (predominantly correct) answer.

For example, if your learner answers: *A cow is an animal and it moos.*

You can reply: *That's great. A cow is an animal that moos.*

Don't draw attention to the alternative you are modeling. Just say it and move on.

6. Most importantly....

Most importantly, make this a FUN experience with your learner!

Learning happens best when our brains are relaxed - not stressed. It is your job to make sure your student's brain stays ready to learn while doing this workbook. Build success upon success and celebrate every small achievement.

LEVEL ONE

DESCRIBING AN OBJECT

COACHING GUIDE LEVEL 1

In this level your learner describes known objects. Your student begins by building up descriptions one feature at a time until he or she can fluently describe an object using 6-12 (or more!) sentences.

Your learner may complete the worksheets orally with you, or may do them independently, with an in-person review when finished. As mentioned in the "How to Coach" section, we believe completing the workbook orally should be your preferred option, where possible. Not only do the skills generalize more easily, you can give immediate feedback and scaffold struggling learners.

As each part of a description is introduced, the workbook provides individual practice so the learner can demonstrate competency in isolation. The skill is then integrated into the learner's descriptions.

If your learner has difficulty with any of the individual steps, consider working on this skill separately and then return to the workbook.

For example, if your learner struggles with identifying the

category/group, you may need to dedicate some time to working on categorization skills.

ADAPTATIONS/EXTENSIONS FOR OLDER LEARNERS.

If your learner is in middle school or higher, add in additional words from their current school work once they have mastered the basics. This will extend their description skills and also consolidate their knowledge of the subject content. It will also reveal knowledge gaps!

For example, if your learner is studying the solar system, ask them to describe words like 'Saturn', 'comet', etc.

When describing something, start by identifying the group or category it belongs to.

For example: *An apple is a fruit.*

Make a sentence that states the group of each item.

A car

A basketball

A hammer

A piano

Coaching Tip: Remember, oral practice is even more valuable than written practice. Get your learner to say the answer in a complete sentence instead of writing it.

Make a sentence that identifies the group of each item.

 Strawberry

Shirt

Sunflower

Mug

Watermelon

Waffle

When describing something, state what it is used for or what it does.

For example: *A plate is used to serve food*

A cow provides milk. / A cow moos.

Make a sentence that describes the purpose of each item.

 A pizza

A cat

A brick

A map

Make a sentence that identifies the purpose or use of each item.

 Ambulance

Pen

Microwave

Slide

Rain boots

Eye

Make a sentence that describes the group and purpose of each item.

For example: *A cow is an animal and it provides milk.*

 Bed

Phone

Ladder

Socks

Coaching Tip: Descriptions tend to be more natural if group comes first. Encourage this with your learner, but don't be pedantic.

Make a sentence that identifies the group and purpose for each item.

Toothbrush

Bottle

Bike tire

Classroom

Rope

Blanket

When describing something, mention what it looks like. You can mention its SIZE, SHAPE and COLOR.

For example: *An apple is red and round.*

A ladder is tall and straight.

Make a sentence that mentions at least two details about the appearance of each item.

A hammer

A car

A piano

A chair

Make a sentence that mentions at least two details about the appearance of each item.

Shirt

Sunflower

Kayak

Watermelon

Waffle

Pillow

Make a description by stating the group, purpose and visual appearance.

For example: *A cow is an animal and it provides milk. It can be black and white and is about the size of a horse.*

Describe the following items mentioning each type of information you have learned. You can use the title of the page as a reminder.

Drill

Ladder

Mountain

Coaching Tip: Expect your learner to have extended processing time as they get all the details out. That is fine!

Describe the group, purpose and visual appearance of each item.

 Bottle

Table

Lawn mower

Roof rack

Nail clippers

River

Describe the group, purpose and visual appearance of each item.

Baseball cap

Knife

Tree

Rain

Rain jacket

Coaching Tip: Are you impressed with how far your student has come? Make sure your learner knows!!

When describing something, mention SOUND, TASTE, FEEL or SMELL - if they are noticeable.

For example: *Old sneakers smell stinky.*

A cat is soft.

Describe each item, mentioning either the taste, smell, feel or sound of the item.

A fish

Candy

A brush

A wet dog

Make a sentence that mentions one or two details about what each item feels, smells, tastes or sounds like.

 Rose

Train

Roast chicken

Pillow

Sand

Coaching Tip: Where appropriate, encourage your learner to give two details. For example, a campfire feels warm and smells smoky.

Describe the objects by stating the group, purpose, visual appearance and any other relevant sensory details.

For example: *A cow is an animal and it provides milk. It can be black and white and is about the size of a horse. A cow has short, smooth fur and it moos.*

Describe each of the following using all the features you have learned.

Skis

Bed

Ladder

Coaching Tip: The re-use of words from previous sections is intentional as it makes the increased challenge more doable.

Describe the objects by stating the group, purpose, visual appearance and any other relevant sensory details.

 Camp fire

Doorbell

Mud

Old Cheese

Sandpaper

When describing something, mention WHERE you usually find it or WHEN you use it.

For example: *A car drives on the road.*

A toothbrush is used in the morning and before bed.

Make a sentence mentioning WHEN or WHERE for each item.

Candy

A brush

A window

A scarf

Make a sentence that mentions WHEN or WHERE.

Computer

Roof

Police Car

Library

Gondola

Moon

Describe the objects by mentioning all the features mentioned in the list above.

For example: *A cow is an animal and it provides milk. It can be black and white and is about the size of a horse. A cow has short, smooth fur and it moos. Cows are found on a farm.*

Describe each of the following.

Bed

Roof rack

Passport

Canoe

Describe each item using all the features listed above.

Keyboard

Wood

Seeds

Desk

Happiness

Coaching Tip: The last example is more challenging. To help with the description, think of how people look/act when they are happy.

When describing something, mention some of its more obvious parts.

For example: *A car has wheels and an engine.*

Make a sentence that describes some of the item's parts.

A book

A window

A microwave

Shoes

A building

Make a sentence that describes some of the parts of each item.

Tree

City

Beach

TV

Tissue Box

Bathroom

Describe the objects by mentioning all the features in the list above.

For example: *A cow is an animal and it provides milk. It can be black and white and is about the size of a horse. A cow has short, smooth fur and it moos. Cows are found on a farm. A cow has four legs, a head and a tail.*

Describe each of the following using each of the features listed in the page title.

 Drill

Pillow

Fireplace

GROUP + PURPOSE + VISUAL + OTHER SENSES +
WHEN/WHERE + PARTS 2

Describe each item using all the features listed above.

 Bus

Screwdriver

Garden

Classroom

Juice box

Homework

When describing something, mention any connection you have or interesting information you know about the item.

For example: *My dad just bought a new car.*

Complete the sentences, mentioning something personal or something you know about the item.

Crutches

Belt

Atlas

Fence

Make a sentence that mentions some additional information about the item.

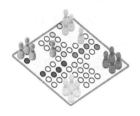 Board game

Surf board

Vacuum cleaner

Hotel

Sun

Umbrella

Describe the objects by mentioning all the features in the list above.

For example: *A cow is an animal and it provides milk. It can be black and white and is about the size of a horse. A cow has short, smooth fur and it moos. Cows are found on a farm. A cow has four legs, a head and a tail. My dad lived on a farm with cows when he was a kid.*

 Vase

Comb

Box

Suitcase

GROUP + PURPOSE + VISUAL + OTHER SENSES +
WHEN/WHERE + PARTS + PERSONAL 2

Describe each item using all the features listed above.

 Snow

Pillow

Chewing gum

Hurricane

Brakes

Doorbell

Describe each item using all the features listed above.

Bath

Beanbag

Scissors

Ice

Rake

Shovel

LEVEL TWO

DESCRIBING A PERSON

COACHING GUIDE LEVEL 2

In this level your student learns to describe people. The worksheets use the same structured approach where the description is built up piece by piece.

The details are adjusted slightly to account for the different requirements of describing people. To summarize:

Group: Male, female, man, woman, boy, girl, teacher, friend, etc.

Purpose (what they do): teaches students, works in a shop, helps me with homework, etc.

Visual Details: Age, hair color, height, clothes style, etc.

Other details: What are they holding, looking at, listening to, etc.

When/Where: Where or when your student encounters them.

Personal Connection or Knowledge: Any other information the learner knows about the person.

. . .

We encourage you to add people from your student's life to the list of people to describe. Think about specific teachers, friends, family members and known people in the community.

When describing someone, start by identifying the gender and approximate age.

You can say: man, woman, boy, girl, old man, young woman, teenager, etc.

For example: *In the picture I see a teenage girl.*

State the gender and approximate age for each person.

IDENTIFY THE GROUP 2

Make a sentence that tells the group of each person.

When describing someone, state what they do or how they are related to you.

For example: *This is a woman and she is a teacher.*

Give a purpose for each person.

Make a sentence that identifies what each of these people do, or how they are related to you.

Extend your description by stating the group and the purpose.

For example: *This is a woman and she is a teacher.*

Give a sentence for each picture.

GROUP + PURPOSE 2

Make a sentence that identifies the group and purpose for each person.

When describing someone, mention what he or she looks like. You can mention HEIGHT, HAIR COLOR/STYLE and CLOTHES.

For example: *She has dark curly hair and is wearing jeans and a T-Shirt.*

Describe the appearance of each person. Mention at least two things.

Describe what each person looks like.

Extend your description by stating the group, purpose and visual appearance.

For example: *This is a picture of a man. He is a fireman and he is wearing a red jacket and black boots. He has short brown hair.*

Describe each person.

Describe the group, purpose and visual appearance for each person.

Describe the group, purpose and visual appearance for each person.

When describing someone, mention other details like what they are holding and what they might hear, smell or taste.

For example: *The man is listening to music on the radio.*

Describe other sensory details for each person.

IDENTIFY OTHER DETAILS 2

Describe at least two additional details for each person that are not related to appearance.

Describe each person by stating the group, purpose, visual appearance and any other relevant details.

For example: *There is a man with blonde hair. He is a scuba diver. He is wearing a wet suit and carrying goggles. He looks like he is all wet.*

Describe the group, purpose, visual appearance and other details of each of these people.

GROUP + PURPOSE + VISUAL +OTHER SENSES 2

Give a description that identifies the group, purpose, visual appearance and other details for each person.

When describing someone, mention WHERE you usually find them or WHEN you see them.

For example: *A doctor works in a hospital.*

I see the dentist when my tooth hurts.

Make a sentence mentioning WHEN or WHERE.

IDENTIFY WHEN AND WHERE 2

Make a sentence that mentions WHEN or WHERE you see this person.

Describe each person by mentioning all the features mentioned in the list above.

For example: *This is a man who is an astronaut. He is wearing a white space suit and is holding his helmet. An astronaut works in space.*

Describe each of the following.

GROUP + PURPOSE + VISUAL + OTHER SENSES +
WHEN/WHERE 2

Describe each person using all the features listed above.

When describing someone, mention any connection you have or interesting information you know about them.

For example: *A sky diver must check their parachute before they jump.*

Mention something personal or something you know about each person.

IDENTIFY PERSONAL 2

Mention something personal or something you know about each person.

GROUP + PURPOSE + VISUAL + OTHER SENSES +
WHEN/WHERE + PERSONAL 1

Describe each person by mentioning all of the features in the list above.

GROUP + PURPOSE + VISUAL + OTHER SENSES + WHEN/WHERE + PERSONAL 2

Describe each person using all the features listed above.

GROUP + PURPOSE + VISUAL +OTHER SENSES +
WHEN/WHERE + PERSONAL 3

Describe each person using all the features listed above.

LEVEL THREE

DESCRIBING AN EVENT

COACHING GUIDE LEVEL 3

In this level your student learns how to describe an event.

The description is built up piece by piece, like in previous levels. The details are adjusted to account for the different requirements of describing an event. To summarize:

Who: What people were involved?

Why: Why were people there?

When/Where: When and where did the situation happen?

Action: What did they do? (beginning, middle, end)

Feelings: What feelings did people have?

Personal Connection or Knowledge: What other information do you know about the situation/event?

Where possible, for each example event, make a connection to a real world equivalent for your student. For example, when it comes to describing a birthday party, ask your learner to describe a specific party that they have attended recently.

We encourage you to add additional events from your student's life to the list of events to describe. Think about weekly activities, what happens at school, and other activities your student participates in.

When describing an event, start by identifying who was there.

For example: *All of Kayla's classmates came to her party.*

Tim went to the beach.

Describe who is at each event.

 Having a barbecue

Playing with a friend

School assembly

Going to visit a friend

Describe who is at each event.

A birthday party

Walking to school

Grocery shopping

Attending a soccer game

Going hiking

Going to get the car repaired

When describing an event, state why the people were there.

For example: *John and Sarah went to the pool to go swimming.*

Liam went to the jetty to see the big new boat.

Describe why people attend each of these events.

Going to the hardware store

Attending music class

Making a phone call

Going to the vet

Describe why people attend each of these events.

 Christmas shopping

Summer holidays

Going to buy shoes

Building a house

Playing with stuffed animals

Planting seeds

Extend your description by stating the Who and the Why of the event.

Alexander went to the mall to buy some new clothes for school.

Describe who participated and why they participated.

Going to the doctor

Making a phone call

Vacuuming

Making breakfast

Describe who participated and why they participated.

Buying a book

Baking a cake

Planning a birthday party

Cleaning the house

Toasting marshmallows

Mowing the lawn

When describing an event, mention WHEN and WHERE it happened.

For example: *My party was at the park last Saturday.*

We went shopping yesterday at the farmer's market.

Describe WHEN and WHERE the event happened.

Going to a pumpkin patch

Going to the beach

Getting a haircut

Shopping for a birthday present for your mom

Describe WHEN and WHERE the event happened.

 Riding a bike

Christmas day

Going to the mall

Valentine's day

Going to a bakery

Cleaning windows

Describe an event by mentioning all the features mentioned in the list above.

For example: *Last Christmas my family went to stay with my grandparents so we could have Christmas together. They live in Florida. We arrived the day before Christmas.*

Describe each event.

Going skiing

Going to a museum

Taking out the trash

Visiting a farm

Describe each event using all the features listed above.

 Catching a bus

Playing at the park

Doing the laundry

Going for a run

Playing a soccer game

Getting in trouble at school

When describing an event, mention what actions happen at the Beginning, Middle and End.

For example: *On Christmas day, we opened presents in the morning, then we visited our neighbors and then we had a big dinner at night.*

Describe what happens at the beginning, middle and end of each of these events.

Making a campfire

Shoveling snow

Painting a picture

Making pizza

IDENTIFY ACTIONS 2

Describe what happens at the beginning, middle and end of each of these events.

 Cooking an egg

Going to a party

Gardening

Playing a board game

Grocery shopping

Describe the event by mentioning Who, Why, When/Where and Actions.

For example: *All my friends came to my birthday party. They came because it was my birthday and I invited them. The party was on Saturday at my house. When everyone came we played some games, then we had cake and pizza. At the end, I opened the presents and said thank-you.*

Describe each of the following events.

Going on a boat

Going to a trampoline park

Coming home from school

Describe each of the following events. Use all the features listed in the heading.

Doing a science experiment

Going to a school concert

Halloween

Cleaning my room

Walking to school

When describing an event, mention how people felt during the event.

For example: *John got mad when Liam took his toy.*

Describe people's feelings during these events. Make sure to use complete sentences.

 Going to a theme park

Going to a movie

Making your bed

Buying new clothes

Describe people's feelings during these events. Make sure to use complete sentences.

Borrowing a book from the library

Playing laser tag

Going to the dentist

Making a sandwich

Planning activities for summer vacation

Describe the events by mentioning all the features mentioned in the list above.

For example: *I went to the dentist today because one of my teeth hurt. The dentist is near my school. I sat in the chair and then the dentist looked into my mouth and did some stuff. Afterwards I got to choose a toy. I was scared at the beginning, but then I felt okay.*

Describe each of the following events.

Going to the zoo

Having a picnic in the back yard

Playing a card game

Playing trains

Describe each event using all the features listed above.

Growing a plant

Building a snowman

Explaining how to eat an orange

Going to a concert

Helping with chores

Looking for a lost toy

When describing an event, mention any additional connection you have or interesting information that you haven't mentioned yet.

For example: *After I finished bowling, I saw a friend from my soccer team.*

Describe something personal or interesting about the following events.

 Visiting my grandparents

Making a fort

Playing hide and seek

Changing a bike tire

Describe something personal or interesting about the following events.

Breaking something expensive

Cleaning up after dinner

Trying on shoes that are too small

Visiting your cousins

Finding something surprising or interesting

WHO + WHY + WHEN/WHERE + ACTIONS + FEELINGS + PERSONAL 1

Describe the events by mentioning all the features given in the list above.

For example: *I went to the dentist today because one of my teeth hurt. The dentist is near my school. I sat in the chair and then the dentist looked into my mouth and did some stuff. Afterwards I got to choose a toy. I was scared at the beginning, but then I felt okay. I think I will be a dentist when I grow up.*

Describe each of the following events.

Playing soccer

Building a sand castle

Doing homework

WHO + WHY + WHEN/WHERE + ACTIONS + FEELINGS + PERSONAL 2

Describe each event using all the features listed above.

Flying a kite

Playing baseball

Playing on the monkey bars

Math class

Playing with a friend

Doing a group assignment at school

WHO + WHY + WHEN/WHERE + ACTIONS + FEELINGS + PERSONAL 3

Describe each event using all the features listed above.

Building a paper airplane

Doing an obstacle course

Playing tennis

Recess time at school

Having a barbecue

BEFORE YOU GO

If you found this book useful, please leave a short review on Amazon. It makes an amazing difference for independent publishers like Happy Frog Press. Just two sentences will do!

Don't forget to look for other workbooks in the **Six-Minute Thinking Skills** series, publishing in 2018 & 2019.

Your learners might also benefit from our **Six-Minute Social Skills series**.

The workbooks in this series build core social skills for kids who have social skills challenges, such as those with Autism, Asperger's and ADHD.

Although numbered, these books can be used in any order.

CERTIFICATE
OF
ACHIEVEMENT

THIS CERTIFICATE IS AWARDED TO

_____

IN RECOGNITION OF

_____

_____   _____

DATE   SIGNATURE

Made in the USA
Las Vegas, NV
08 November 2024

11374775R00056